The Literate Detective

&

Other Crimes

The Literate Detective & Other Crimes

PAUL SCULLY

Published by Bonfire Books,
753-755 Nicholson Street
Carlton North, VIC 3054, Australia
info@bonfirebooks.org
www.bonfirebooks.org

ISBN 978-0-6457768-8-1

A catalogue record for this book is available
from the National Library of Australia

Cover: C Grimmer

Acknowledgements

I would like to thank the editors of the following publications and online poetry forums for publishing the following poems:[1]

"A Defiant Cosmos", *The Borough*, Issue 1, Southern Spring 2024
"A Griefing of Crows", *Canto Planetario: Hermandad en La Tierra*, Vol. II, Asia y Europa, HC Publishing, 2023.
"Amniocentesis", *Anthology of Australian Verse 2023*, Bonfire Books, 2023.
"An All Stations Train", *Love: 2023 ACU Prize for Poetry*, Australian Catholic University, 2023.
"Any Way the Wind Blows", *Anthology of Australian Verse 2023*, Bonfire Books, 2023.
"Bamboo Spine", *Resilience*, Mascara Literary Review, Ultimo Press, 2022.
"Bashō in the Suburbs*", Return Ticket from Sydney to Bistrita: A Lyrical Carousel Between the Antipodes*, Australian Romanian Academy Publishing, 2021.
"Campsie Street, Campsie in the Decade of Love", *Resilience: 2021 ACU Prize for Poetry*, Australian Catholic University, 2021.
"*Cinema Grotesquerie*", *The Borough*, Issue 1, Southern Spring 2024
"Distant Discourse", *Anthology of Australian Verse 2023*, Bonfire Books, 2023.
"In the Mind of Lithe Evil", *Guide to Sydney Crime*, Meuse Press, 2022.
"Lost for Words (Intamooga/Black-Footed Tree Rat", *Return Ticket from Sydney to Bistrita: A Lyrical Carousel Between the Antipodes*, Australian Romanian Academy Publishing, 2021.
"Mind Stunts", Parts 1, 2 and 3, *Australian Poetry Anthology*, Vol. 9, 2021-22, Australian Poetry, 2021.
"The Detective's Almanac", *The Borough*, Issue 1, Southern Spring 2024
"The Firebirds", *Natural History and Historians, Science Write Now*, Edition 6, https://www.sciencewritenow.com/read/natural-history-and-historians/the-firebirds.
"The Literate Detective (Excerpts)", *Dumbóvá*, Newcastle Poetry Prize Anthology, Hunter Writers' Centre, 2024.
"The Post-Modern Problem with Trolleys and Footbridges", *Hermes 2016*, Issue 110, Sydney University Union, 2016.
"Wink", Philosophy, *Rabbit: a journal for non-fiction poetry*, Issue 18, 2016.
"Yellow Tailed Cockatoos on Culburra Beach", *Canto Planetario: Hermandad en La Tierra*, Vol. II, Asia y Europa, HC Publishing, 2023.

---

[1] In some instances I have changed the poems slightly since their earlier publications. In at least one instance, I have changed the poem's title. "In the Mind of Lithe Evil" was published as "Lithe Evil". "Mind Stunts", Parts 1, 2 and 3 was published as "Phenomenology".

TABLE OF CONTENTS

My thanks to Les Wicks for seeding the idea of "The Literate Detective" though his COVID call-out for True Crime poems.

As always, thanks also to Judith Beveridge and her redoubtable poetry group for inspiration and insightful feedback.

My gratitude, too, to my brother, Kevin Scully, for poetic fellowship across the seas.

The Literate Detective

The Detective's Almanac

None of trench coat, fedora, deerstalker, priestly vestments,
nuns' habits, an inscrutable Caucasian posing in yellowface,
   a sou'wester and battered jeep or waddling spats spells
 investigation, so too this thesaurus bypasses the upturned bottle
   and marriage havoc, those tropical tropes, but embraces gumshoe.
   Accoutrements don't measure mind. The city may be naked, the dragnet

   trawled through low-life alleyways, demeanour made matter-of-fact
in the matter of fiction, but observation is never wanton,
   slogged feet may stumble, but trample on, and minutiae adhere
to the sub-conscience–lightning bolts pierce the ether as often
   as moonlight is pickled viridian. Facts beget premise and more facts,
the human is always connective tissue and McGuffins are best left

   onscreen. Death is labile and numerous, harm and hurt a chasm,
theft a cloying absence, omission the greater part of untruth,
   emotions wisely forensic and guilt eternal, though necessarily
a found object in our trade. When the case is solved, the file sutured
   shut, in exhaustion and sometimes error, I have inventory
enough of eyes and teeth, revenge is more prison than sweet harbour.

I Blame Cluedo

No Damascus, no horse-toppling
                              moment, no light haloing the hillside, no significant

astronomy of any kind; more my brain gone to custard, debating whether Colonel
Mustard deserved to be busted, or whether it was Professor Plum who shot
the gun, concealed beneath his academic gown until the kismet moment.
In early gestation I shunned books and films as if they were soups to be ladled
into my fevered brain, a description my Mum used as she patted my head

and pinched my cheeks.
                              I needed grit, not nutrition, the knowing was palpating

hands, pavement-thudding feet, live or near live tissue, all manner of doing,
even in play. True crime arrived later with a plot-charting and re-enactment value, texts
crammed my study as I careered towards policing, first in unform, then in Fletcher Jones
suits, though never topped by a trilby or pork pie hat, obituaries and eulogies
now case-research, my ever-present notepad—names, places, times, actions—

a breviary for contemplating evidence,
                              a songbook for the dance of proof.

The Academy

An alien among the boosters, the rogues, the defiantly
compliant, in shy concert with the anxious and ungainly,
once lofty standards shrunk for inclusion and a dearth
of the willing tall, weeks of fitness merging into martial arts,
whisks of law and psychology, a sampling of forensics, prison
visits, cloistered evenings and clone-drill marching,
then graduation hats aloft my ticket of leave, or at least release
into the regiments of the flung together. The criminally young
stripped for imaginary drugs, the leg-swept indigenous,
the outlier scorn, the arrogations all on daily show, yet the honest
artisan also labours there, the monitor of body counts
and road carnage, the searcher for the lost child, the bastion
of outward calm when threat or distress teems through our pores—
this the nursery of a future sleuth, its swaddling ambivalence.

The Crowded Streets

The headlights blur in the reflection
of oily residues on a well-driven road,
my eyes seek the refuge of the shadows beyond,
my snoring senior a drone in my ear,
his waking brusqueness a goad
to add distance to my natural reserve;
what lessons survive his ego require the wand
of the subconscious to emerge.

We uniforms rarely choose our arrivals,
whether there be drums of war or dance, beaten
or exultant spirits, resentment or relief;
tonight a domestic swill,
deluge drinking, imprecations heathen
and devout, the well-trodden staircase to outburst,
violence: blame, shame or omission the motif
of the morning to come.

The moon-sun shift-change tugs
at the ragged ends of fitful sleep and meals taken
in reverse, and people taste more bitter
even in their customary dosage.
They are a cocktail, served still, stirred or shaken,
but mostly tend their lives in gentle anonymity
and come to know us in a world out-of-kilter
or out of options.

Donning a Suit

My uniform began to imprint like a second skin,
my mind risked retuning by its martial cells, in prospect
a shrunken horizon, the ceding of self,
mercy left to wither in the grayscaling of my dream.

I reclaimed it by committing to the detective exams
with only a callow career to prosecute my cause.
My senior and station chief declined to support
my application, seeing more froth than cream.

Doggedness is a mire or ladder, depending on its aim …
For me it eroded my supervisors' resistance
and the extra years spent preparing cushioned
my ride, the vigil pending assignment a twilight.

No Mod Squads for suburban detectives—flares more
distress than trousers—their ordinary citizen garb
bespoke another uniformity, the right to question worn
with a swagger, but scant sign of that rarer bird, insight.

Graduating to Murder

For detectives murder is jagged breath, febrile kisses, seduction, la crime de la crime. It means no more daily fare of break-ins, bag snatching and fence-line feuds, return there only by assignment, with special expertise loud and lurid as you re-enter reception.

Competition for places is a ruckus: seniority, time in the queue, keeping your head high but not gun-sight lofty, merit, favouritism, inclusion criteria nowadays and deep aquifers of patience. As with becoming a detective, the petitioner must court the senior and station chief for succour and prepare for multiple round-trips; mine was threefold.

Day one, posted to the outer ring of the pack, a curdling shame as I pined for a call-out–also when I practised killing thoughts–though I knew I would mostly thicken the file with routine facts, observer statements and unneighbourly suspicions, a thoroughness sometimes stinted when the blood ran hot.

This frisson darkened the longer I knotted an intricate death into my expectant brow but glinted occasionally with shards of sympathy and reflections on evil as the tally of simple homicides mounted. In time the dingo howl of duty and my pledges to justice and the common good all jostled forward. The moral compass may have no feet but it lengthens your stride.

My First Corpse

A ping on my skin   hail   my mind transported to my child
self   that rain could be bladed   water's benevolence
forever tainted for me   I had never known flood   Drops
now arc from my umbrella's ribs down my neck as I change
hands   the moment reasserted   Death's mercery veiling
the face   obscuring gender   a colleague cuffs my back
Ready?   I plant my foot in nervous resolve   ease into a squat
will my hand to still its tremors   A woman   an unremitting
likelihood   my breath struggles to contain itself
a fate voided of purpose   mine now to requite   her eyes
shuttered   a sallow pallor despite the mottle of bruises
I take a full inventory of violence   cleaved lip   occluded eye
sockets   forehead abrasions   as if ploughed into a hard surface
chafed ears   a corona of blotches around the neck
hand imprints   acid scours my throat   forensics for the rest
questions that will never know a first person response

My First Solve

Through the window of the detectives' room, the sky was a sliver
on fine days, an end-stop on gloomy, the room itself a fug
of instant coffee and wildebeest armpits whatever the meteorology
or shirt print, the desktops always tussocked with unemptied ashtrays.

There were no incident rooms back then, no sticky tape or blu tack
visuals, no marker pen confabulations, just pocket notebooks we flipped
lengthwise as we decanted our measures of misbehaviour, squashed
into chairs that subverted most human shapes into question marks,

and waited for the assemblage of a melancholic or ambitious superintendent,
the one mechanical in the way of a broken-tooth typewriter, the other
prey to the logic of a gazelle, the pressure to assign blame insistent hailstones
on iron roofing whoever led the case. A first lesson emerged: look

for the forced meld when the pieces are too tongue-and-groove
or dowel perfect; the scars of a made unison are hidden from view.
(The awkwardly aligned had yet to find a light bulb in me.)
It fell to me to unpick the case chronology–a locksmith become safe

cracker–its logistical elegance such that each act and journey was deftly
tagged one to another, fore and aft, and any delay or mishap would scuttle
our suspect's alibis. As we probed the margins, our suspect resisted,
wavered, appended and revised, the thread of concoction unspooled

and he booked a saloon passage to the dock. Midnight pondering:
a half-truth punctures less easily than a bald-faced, or even bearded, lie;
past patterns frame the cross-hairs and they lock onto the obvious suspect
Occam's-razorly, indecently almost, whither our acquiescence or query?

The Days and Weeks Swell into Months and Years

Buses, trains, uniforms are sprinkled among the drowsy
when serving at transport friendly stations, detectives a dentured hen rarity,
taxis occasionally, uber aeons yet, carpooling when shifts and affability make friends,
the solo drive most common, the excuse odd hours and end time
unpredictability, but the spatial stare, a glimpse
of the void, the creative aloneness of hands on the wheel, even as the radio
might toll away the minutes and miles, these are treasures of the day not easily forsaken.
The short wave in the squad car, taken home only selectively, fizzes with static,
call-outs, orders—all argot and palsied grammar—while staccato

conversation punctures what silence remains. It is mostly shop,
the personal a rare tangent, a scudding stone, the moody trove unbreached.
When a case is closed, there is fanfare or an exasperated or treasury stalemate.
For ones where effort never flags but leads merely follow, time might
expose new morsels despite our vulturine diligence.
There are days when we juggle cyclones, others when we are marooned
in an empty freight train diverted to a desert siding spur-line or are pantomime players
in an endless season. We are prone to formulae and procedures,
and names can become like car number plates

to those not neurally dredged by vision of the corpse.
They label this survival or objectivity's necessary distance. Case-deep,
I try to consecrate a moment each day to blood-and-breath-sensing the victim,
the hollowness of the erasure from the portrait on the mantlepiece,
the turn of the calendar rupturing the wound anew.
I also seek displacement in the gym, temporary by the cast
of my mind, in the pool. I have tried the bar but found it a pitfallen resort.
While my headwaters swell behind me, I am becalmed in these seething plains,
blind to the sea and the tide that will carry me there.

The Ship Lists and Sinks

Sirocco, Harmattan, this furnace wind of a dream shreds
me into wilted reeds, my wakefulness as weary as sleep.

Nightmare, daymare, it is no respecter of time, nor
the adage's healing properties.
                        The dream has prismed

into a delta, the one person variously protagonist, character,
caricature, chimera, within and across the rivulets. The scenes

shape-shift and colour-morph at will, the narratives are involuted,
my memories mosaics.
                      Habit, instinct, discomfort in the tropics

of self ... I raided stationery for a case folder, but paused
at the title square: the cradle and flashbacks the crime scene,

the offence to raddle unrecognised images and to disquiet me,
victim, witness, abettor and sleuth? Freud, Adler and Jung

counsel that clues abound in sex, family and totems. They ransacked
the Greek myths and Latin dictionaries for labels, as if to ennoble

their theories, but they offer only fog for crime, the lives it mires,
their clotted horizons the unredeemed purgatory of a shadowed sun.

I have taken the dream as a sign, the end of my enlistment
in the penumbra is mete; I must turn the sods of another reality.

Scrapbook

1.   Down by Lane Cove River, 1963

A muzzled greyhound loped through
a lover's lane Sunday morning beside
a spent condom of a river, the low lying
air weighted by a chemical fug.
Two corpses with loins exposed strewn
a stagger's distance from the square
of carpet lain decorously beside
the car's open door; the dog's trainer,
his wiry frame constructed from a lifetime's habits,
bequeathed the woman a cardboard
modesty and redeployed the man's suit coat
before scarpering into the self-concern
that had nursed him since a childhood
boating accident not far from where
he now walked. Her rifled handbag
littered a riverbank upstream.
Two boys gambolling for golf balls
inherited the job of calling the police
after gulping out the news of purple lips
and seeping blood to their parents.

A tryst of scientists, both from swing door
marriages, itself a seam of suspicion
for stern detectives in an otherwise age,
but their spouses proved impenetrably
innocent. Other scientists assayed tissues
for toxins, though not the hydrogen sulphide
of the later theory, none leached free.
The tissues were discarded, the verdict
circulatory failure. The Cold War
was unthawed, Reds fomented under beds,
his physics were new terrain—masers
and radio astronomy—her husband
a Communist and ASIO sponge,
the *Spycatcher* author claimed Russian
recruitment, a friend that the Americans
feared contamination of their atomic silence,

disposal their remedy. The coroner
withheld evidence from his own inquest,
divining stale entrails now our scant resort.

2.   The Magnetic Drill Gang, 1978

A flat lake Thursday ahead for Murwillumbah, any breeze
an oven's breath, exertion a wound of sweat even this early,
night draining into waking whispers, shadows skulk
in the laneway that is back-story to the main street,
an end-of-shift security guard forages for peaceful confirmation,
stumbles upon an open door at the bank of all places.
His eggshell steps gasp him to the vault, where a second,
studied eye snares the drill hole. All else is stickle-and-pin tidy.
He radios HQ and unleashes the police, the media
and speculation that spools unrequited still, though an aged crim
has staked a claim.

                              The thieves had stalked the town,
gauged its rhythms and tics, their onslaught timed for the night
an armoured truck flush with payroll and cash for pension
day had swollen the vault. The lore does not record the manner
of knowing, as if fact were divination enough, but recounts
a circular electro-magnet, a diamond-tipped drill, a medical
cystoscope peering through the hole into the lock's tumblers,
a wand of sorts to unfuddle them, which they then jammed,
an exit excavation through the ceiling to the second floor,
in direct line of sight from the Imperial's front bar, wall
intervening, with drinkers' cars parked in bays astride the bank.

Chubb technicians could not retumble the lock, council
sledgehammers and pneumatic drills conscripted as a mean resort,
success and mayhem in equal measure. A deduced circular economy
of the theft of a Chubb safe in Melbourne, rehearsal heists,
identikits of men seen in the street nine thirty-ish, a Holden
panel van recalled in the vicinity and the Gold Coast
a theorised launch pad and bolt hole complete the narrative:
genius now bowdlerised into tea towels and stubby holders.

3.   Lady Leatherface: "Never to be Released", 2000

a frying pan to the
head after a late
night return

an attempt to strangle her first husband
for the sin of sleep after merely three
wedding night consummations

an iron to the head and
scissors in his entrails
for other infractions

A pet dingo pup's throat slit in front of her
new beau for maintaining the apartment he
rented before meeting her

      I have gouged this entry, our first female lifer,
        from her file, flesh for flesh. I've had to fillet
some of the gristle from her crimes lest their barbs embed themselves
beneath my shadow skin, even in archive. The headlines scalped a name
        from a horror movie to crown her ferocity. Here she
        will simply be she, she who scorched my kidneys

        with the dry ice of evil. I will also leave her pre-history
        to whelk in its own bloody sump and start at her second John,
the victim in her imprisonment, the first an eventless exception
by her standards. On her wounding way to the dead John, she had
        mounted a display case of knives above her bed,
        an icon in worship of fate gifting her a dream job

        as a pig slaughterman. John II had refused
        to marry her but stayed from dread for his life
and his children's. For this she framed him for theft and stabbed him
in the chest. Home from the late shift as usual on his death night,
        a rugged fuck at her insistence, a shower, then blessed rest,
        only to be woken by a knife piercing his ribs and siphoning

the air from his lungs. A havoc of 37 blows ended his momentary flight.

Here, with a ginger tread, I note her cutlery at its eviscerating work, a chef-aping gloss on her abattoir skills, labelled plates for his children and a blizzard of pills, after which she collapsed beside his remains and was found there the next morning.

I cannot erase what I have omitted; I waver in a bardo between numb and alert, between shield and sword. I must remember to breathe.

4.   In the Mind of Lithe Evil[2], 2024

'Shiv", Shiva the Destroyer, shiver
—a sonata of spine and fear—
I have loved this word waywardly,
the sleek espionage of how it
infiltrates a ribcage, punctures
a lung, the sectioning of an artery,
lengthwise or transversely, each
a delight in terminal craftmanship.
(I am also fond of "stiletto".)
My first sallies were rehearsals
in pain, a buttock in an ATM queue,
an eye to an escaping corner, an arm
clutching a backpack strap
in a train entranceway, flight
through a just-in-time door.
I experimented with hidey-holes
until a sleeve-seam presented itself
as home for a wiry scabbard
and I devised a means of shaking
the shiv free, unobtrusively. Now
I cut a fine figure prowling
the laneways and night shadows.

---

[2] https://www.9news.com.au/national/melbourne-news-woman-fighting-for-life-three-others-in-hospital-after-stabbing-spree-across-melbourne/0f366d55-107f-4cd5-a18d-85446c774de6.

Clusters

Amniocentesis

1. The Call of the Caul

The midwife's Adriatic mane, which cascades over her nape
when she frolicks, now tufts through her cap,
pearls of sweat braid an arc across her brow,
a shape that opens the room to the sky somehow,
and all that beckons beyond, her mind drifts to myrrh,
frankincense, gold, the star-bound cameleers; then awe
rounds her mouth as she massages the newborn from the sac
that envelops her like some in utero bubblewrap for her haulage
into breath and nestles her in the swaddling rug
swagged as a homely token in the birthing suite.
Were the midwife's hands not steeped in these beginnings,
they would sign the crucifixion about her bodily planes,
for the daily miracle her profession avails
and the portent of greatness her grandmother's myth alerts
her to–Charlemagne, Napoleon, destructive men, first
among the heritage conveyed; this tot more sweetly fated,
she prays, remembering the rite of paper adumbrated
with the caul, and kept as a relic or shadow specimen,
and how sailors supposedly bid for fragments as talismans
against the deep, for those so born would never drown.

2. A Bird in a Pocket

Aloft, the sky is its own language; words require
landing gear to assay the vastness, to mimic
the senses, whether upweighted by thermals,
buffeted by contrary wafts, deliriously unwired
from the tow-craft, or cosseted in the cockpit. We fossick
for metaphors, birds take flight, but dermal
feathers and motile wings orbit them
beyond a glider's geo-station; the slipstream,
the wayward and carefree share an interlude,
though the need for planning and preparation intrudes
upon their complacency. Perhaps the space-suited
embryo in the amniotic sac inside the womb

best reprises the tissular yet shielding frame
that roosts the pilot in the firmament, intuited
as a greater mother than Earth by we who swoon
with parallactic lust at the cosmos, its very name.

3. The Self-Satellite

The world condensed into syllabic bullets, parsed
into magazines, clingwrapped and grenaded
onto our stoop—well, more likely to the top
of the drive these days, if at all, or next door
when the radar is jammed by inattention—
by a car window arm made robotic by daily spars
with delivery. Each report descends a graded
slalom from fact, that redoubt of the almost sure, with props
for comedy, bile or faux-insight, causing the footsore
to remove their shoes for the pebble sensed within.
There are days when I want to sever the umbilicus
and drift off in my amniotic sac like a satellite
gone rogue, the world that bauble in the capsule window
as I churn metaphors into soup. When I rebead the abacus
on my return to gravity, the thresher is my respite,
discernment, judgment, excision the blades I employ.

4. The Divided Magistrate

*Stipendiary Magistrates and justices of the peace do not robe, other than in NSW where they
have worn a black robe over normal business attire since 2005 - Wikipedia.*

A persona hung in a wardrobe, the dry cleaner's plastic sheath
slithered round it like an amniotic sac, though more wreath
than chrysalis given her mood, the robe's black drape restored
to the elevation of judgment by an edict engorged
with hauteur, grit-ignorant, that had slugged her with the Sisyphean
awakening she no longer wanted to play Solomon's ape,
that would demote her from swayback to spine-ruptured
hypocrite if she laboured on. Like the wisest advocate,
she had long repealed the myth of justice, seen it fade
before her in the eyes of the drugged and the born poor, the parade
of the alienated, at mind's tether-end, the true native, had decoded

deterrence into its elemental avoidance, the unbarred alternatives loaded and scanty, the outcomes predestined. Yet their fate should she resign?

Mind Stunts

1. Foreboding

Impeded light, an air-pocket
in the room's high corner, a sudden breeze
across my unshaven chin, an echo
ghosts every sound, my mind rakes
recent encounters for peripheral eyes
or gestures that might have accosted
my self-absorption, the page before me
poised for a pointless third perusal,
the unborn rustle at my shoulder craves a name.

2. Premonition

The road slick with evening's retreat,
the usual traffic glacier, a level crossing
sign hovers above the verge on the climb
to the traffic lights on Malvern Avenue.
Once it registers, I swivel to recapture
the image, but find only columned
emptiness. Later that morning
a random internet search opens onto
a trainspotters' almanac, an attachment
listing 20 years of level crossing accidents,
my breakfast eggs now a sump
that repeats on me. I scour the newspapers
from that time hence, haunt
the radio dial for the latest bulletins.

3. Déjà Vu

Curtains bunched and ruffled, stripes
of oblique light through the casement window
accent a single colour in the shade-dun
pattern, a tie or scarf I once owned perhaps.

My feet find their steps as if in a dance,
as if preceding me, I mime my friend's greeting
to the syllable, welcoming as yesterday.

4. Mirage

Distance on the bitumen is rectangles
of shifting sameness, a javelin runway
west, acid-harsh gibber and ochre
to the north, a pocket of remotest blue,
yet lakes somehow lather the vista,
lapping makeshift foothills
and a pool-shimmer on the road
far ahead. I am a thirsty fool.

5. "Hallucination"

Deft undulations of sand
for an unforgiving sacrum, my neck
knots the bow of a peanut pillow,
the book floats to my chest
like an accordion bird
as the clouds convocate
in my eyes, sun-slit arrows
and splinters are momentary
other voices, wisps become
sparks, whorls, helixes and curlicues
cavort, the cloud cotton chalk-coloured
and cadmium, denim and fuchsia,
the sky now an enveloping lung,
its breath an incubator, a lament,
floral-tinted in the eddies that catch
my whiskers, recommitting
to this finely-grained earth
a sensate light year away.

6. On Waking from a Dream

Revellers clump in corners, beneath
mantelpieces, streaky, resinous plumes filter
through doorways, words without conversation,
the music swings between surge and drone,
boom and echo, my ears are gramophone horns,
my eyes gold lamé buttons, a slit tunic banners
my iridescent flesh.
                  The alarm wails,
I fade upright, my head swims with body heat,
stomach acids bite at my throat, I clutch my tunic
tassels together in pyrrhic modesty, arrive at
pyjamas, smoke a nostril memory, music an arcing
beneath sound, "Whose party was it, anyway?"

Apophenia

1. "Signs and Symbols"[3]

One aged stammer-step after another, a welcome
wheeze at the traffic lights, cigarettes still notching
his breath despite many years' abandonment, bone-rattle
of a train to a far-flung suburb, a mustard-and-sauce hued
bus to the sanatorium, a more reliable term, he avers,
than the modern "facility", more ellipsis than aid
to understanding, reflection the curse of this weekly duty,
which noun impales him and slurs an impasto of guilt
over every worrisome thought when he is refused
permission to sit with his son after an attempted suicide
a few days ago—he hadn't been told … his son to whom
every act and fact, jubilant or sombre, is a circling,
a cipher, an accretion to the theme-scape of his life
… late that night, after a diver's-boot trudge home,
a telephone call, and every few nights thereafter, a shredded voice
gouging out a plea for Remy, not his son's name,
the father's weary first disavowal, his layering frustration
unavailing … he declares to his orphic caller
he has decided he must remove his son from care.

2. A City of Bats

An alpine school bus, its yellow now mustard-hued,
evening ebbing into the crackle-glow of fires
lining a rutted, dust-spawned Congolese track,
circlings of tamping, sloughing feet, a drum-tattoo
metronome, a new pygmy king, we hear, jubilation
shared as we alight into the sweat, embrace, shuffle
and depart. Next morning, after a late night subdued
by reflection on our lordly encounter, we turn north
toward limestone caves, a species undistinguishable

---

[3] The title of a short story by Vladimir Nabokov from which I have borrowed the narrative arc of this poem.

by geography but whose formations, viewed
through slanted, hooded lenses, propose *les similitudes*:
the Eiffel Tower, l'Arc de Triomphe, the dome
of Sacré Coeur, De Gaulle's nose, the doughy Mitterand
jowls, colonial barbs that snag a memory still.
Bats hang like seedpods from the cavern walls
and ceilings, tactile graffiti, and skitter through
the aerial boulevards of this cityscape, giving lie
to the Francophilia the guides feel compelled
to peddle to visitors and locals alike.

3. Stratocumuli

Masses of pillow-soft cloud, a Pangaea, Gondwanaland,
supercontinents aloft against a cobalt-tinting-steel
backdrop, a forever-scape that lures the freed mind
into luscious delusion … we esteem white as if always sacred,
wisping into an Indian triangle, a Cape York lance,
an Italian boot, a Finnish sliver, with fraying borders
and migrant tendrils, but the more sombre and grittier hues
have a murky sentience and also court reflection:
a celestial cud, the sky the orphic fourth stomach
of an other-worldly presence, portents of some fate-
sick or human-wrought doom; a gestating shadow-self,
a prolapse of unstarred space, an archipelago
in a turbid sea … one is a scudding stone, the other
a diving bell, one a song of expansion,
the other a dirge or lament, one mostly beyond self
and farsighted, the other the searchlight of the inward gaze.

4. The Texas Sharpshooter

Link is able to blast a fusillade of pistol-shot
into his barn-side, a Colt, by family statute, rebutting the saying,
but this constellation of pellets portends an expanding
universe, not the sun of marksmanship, stoking white-hot
indignation, so he gouges out the far-flung slugs
and daubs target circlings in jubilant and sombre
hues until he finds a cluster for the centre-spot
of the bullseye, paint bristle-sharp lest his deception

leap from the wood … a drone sighting,
a faulty mobile signal, an interrupted internet, not-
withstanding news of a routine outage, leave him fraught,
wary round phone towers, conspiracy kisses his lips.
Mature reflection is stillborn, lends him no grace.
Passers-by give him more girth than his barbed wire
stature deserves, tune out the tectonic discontent
rumbling beneath his breath and consort
through traded glances, a currency of wariness
equal to Link's—the story-scapes that bind us to memory
may not be the ones our mind-spinnerets manufacture.

Ekphrasis, or Thereabouts

1. Hue and Cry

After listening to an interview with David Coles, Master Paint Maker

His eye revelled in the panther's indigo   His gaze plotted
        the dapple of ochres in the leopard's camouflage   then   somersaulted
into the parrot's cardinal and myrtle   an amber   a goldenrod   perhaps

        unvoiced in that inrush of beauty   His retinal antennae   coded
nuance within pattern   but his hand baulked at the pittance the standard palette
    offered   so he plunged   headlong   into the torrents of the past

that tumble of stones wherein First Nations draped caverns with silhouettes
        a scale insect   the cochineal   connived at Reubens' red   shavings
of lapis lazuli sutured ultramarine into Mary's robe   Turner steeped

        his Indian yellow in the urine of mango-fed cows   Van Gogh
projected chromium into his visions of the night sky   Paris Green savoured
        arsenic   and its ancestor Scheele's Green   confessed to Monet's blindness

after he had divined tin-violet from *plein air*   bone char coaxed black into the light
        and Tyrian purple crowned a predator   a sea snail   while the Dutch
blanched farm ordure with lead and vinegar   His primary school atlas came to mind

how ghost colonies tinted the land masses   how the flags of independence
        must have recast the globe   his attraction to the negative space of oceans
the ley lines of latitude longitude sea currents and wind systems   There was a tidal zone

Pigment   between thought and brush stroke   this   a domain   called to him

2. Bandaged Beauty

Frida Kahlo Exhibition, Sydney Festival, January 2023

In a barrio-catacomb cut away from sandstone–we discover
on our exit the excavation scars on the rockface carry
a seer's imprint–the nearby harbour washes through my ears
like a drum-brush. We enter via a Mexican altar, skulls grin
among the flowers and candles and death are as much theatre
as sacrament; beyond a second door immersion in the beauty
of fracture, where pain cleaves truer than blood or breath,
is the rift-line of each pinned joint, each misshapen limb,
each serrated tendon, wild in her frozen face, while her passions
whorl and cavort around a central image, sometimes singular,
sometimes dualling. Hers is an art of the kernel self, not the barrage
of dreams some attribute to the company she sometimes kept,
neither plaint nor boast, always reflexive, always resplendent,
even when darksome, a humming-bird, fragile, fierce.

3. The Dremel's Edge

Cressida Campbell Exhibition, National Gallery of Australia, January 2023

Fugues: the hallway haloed by her dead husband,
the smothered scuff of his moccasins on the timber
floor, the reflection caught in the pane opposite the sofa
where she reads or the work-a-day reclines into evening–
the world's sprites and shadows are suborned into
mirror-reverse light–all panting for a plywood likeness,
charcoal skeleton and the dremel's edge, the unguents
of watercolour, libations poured across paper and paint,
the tattoo unpeeled as a second skin, the delicate crops
of mosaic unevenness, their querying contours,
a lesser truth should she paint direct to canvas.

Resilience

1. Campsie Street, Campsie in the Decade of Love

Mum loaded up the Holden station wagon on the all-too-frequent
    shopping days seven children imposed on the week; her safety-alert
eyes hogged the road ahead, as if the red brick-and-tile and weatherboard
    "homesteads", their trimmed verge-moustaches, and the courthouse
and police station that presided over the halfway point to the shops
    did not exist. For about a year, though, her peripheral vision snagged
on a young man, the ructions of the age meaningless to his stilted joints
    and the rictus of muscle spasms and torsioned tendons. In the backseat,
the yet-to-schools formed a tetchy train or querulous mire, depending
    on the weather, while an older, pimply lump might be saddled
in the front for packhorse duties and brother-and-sister wrangling.
    We probably more remarked the man's birthplace than the way
he propped himself on walking sticks and clutched at fenceposts
    as he willed movement into his limbs in the slow-motion-rocking
that accumulated half-steps away from his front gate and tore pausing
    breaths from his marrow, the prayer that petitioned any god
who might listen–faith wears livery, mercy is ecumenical–Mum
    would have mouthed a rough-cast rosary along with him. Days,
weeks and months melted the permafrost, a makeshift-enough litheness
    began to ghost his gait and propelled him to the end of the block,
then beyond, and back again. He might never reclaim the vaulting athlete
    of his scampering boy-mind but his progress was sufficiently ardent
for Mum to whisper to the steering wheel, "I admire that young man".

2.   Bamboo Spine[4]

A barely corrugated cane swollen into its own thicket,
its core calcium, unlike the pithy scaffolding on HK skyscrapers
and its confetti of lives in tempest winds. A hollow
metaphor nonetheless, lending appearance only, an image
to be passed over, the spinal cane more likely to snap
than bend, though it stoops, sometimes almost right-angularly
as when a Jain priest shepherds brethren insects away
from undiscriminating feet.
                              The bamboo bearer beats
a two monthly pilgrimage to the clinic, where the oracular
cannula channels a biological ghost to prevent the bearer's system
gnawing on itself, and joins a stoic chorus of like arms, joints
and souls, while doctors and nurses mill caringly in the hospital vortex.

All the while the planets hold to elliptical orbits, the sun calls
the bearers to rise with it, to chop wood, hew stone and carry water,
to rest or bandage when the weight overwhelms or bleeds,
without the promise or prospect of skyhook or light bulb—
dream, prayer or quietude ventures into other worlds—but hopeful
of one moment extending into another, and another,
and aware that you cannot ford the same stream twice.

---

[4] A "bamboo spine" is a term used to describe the appearance of a spine fused over its full length by ankylosing spondylitis, an auto-immune illness.

On the Wing

1.   A Griefing of Crows

a caucus at a carcass
scions of carrion
unnatural   we label
their plenty murder
we adopt black
as our cloth of loss
but recoil at the sable
gleam of the wheeling
columns   oblivious
they might form
a warning bell tower
that tolls in raucous
swollen keening
diminutions of flock
the danger of place

2.   Yellow-Tailed Cockatoos at Culburra Beach

this isthmus of gum trees
    isolated by squalls of humankind
    buffeted by their trade winds of loss
the stand near the main beach
    similarly marooned
I lie some days on the foot-snaring track
    close my eyes
    settle the muffling surf
    into a back-wash
tune my ear-radar to their call
    that creak
    that soprano yodel fragment
    words have such slender purchase
let my eyes trail sound
    until I catch the birds' wry curiosity
    their roosting joy
    a glint of tail-flare

3.   The Firebirds

Facing uphill on a morning that has just shaken
off the dew, the lyrebird co-opts gravity
as she backheels a storm into the scrub flotsam.
She stumbles on and voices a chainsaw lodged deep
in her gorge in the same motion. She engineers
a compost from the leaves, twigs and banksia cones,
the chrysalides and shed skins, sifting and shifting it,
mounding it, gouging out catacombs and sanctuaries
for snakes and lower-slung vertebrates. Only wildfire
rivals her in upheaval, a dozen skips' worth
per year, yet fire breeds more cold-bloodedly
where her husbandry has not prevailed.

~

While the galahs and Major Mitchells flock
to sanctuary, at the fire-front, the perching
opportunism of black kites and brown falcons
has vision only for the single-minded flurry
of insects, lizards and small mammals under the whip
of flame. Should their appetites surmount this bounty,
the hawks may pilfer an ember and freight
it to a more distant part of the savanna where they
will stoke another oven in the grasslands. The science
journals are only now the equals of the lore-men.

Sage Advice

1.   Little Analects

Not every day will be a moonwalk,
much as our fable-seeking selves might will it so.
The smaller in scale also have their triumphs—
in essence, the mosaic turns on its tesserae,
the infinitesimal is infinity in miniature,
and an ember glows on the bleakest day:
there is a riddle to life.
The witless sage consigned this to a sea bottle
before it slipped from memory.

Runes whispering in the clouds.

Before it slipped from memory,
the witless sage consigned this to a sea bottle—
there is a riddle to life
(and an ember glows on the bleakest day):
the infinitesimal is infinity in miniature,
in essence, the mosaic turns on its tesserae;
the smaller in scale also have their triumphs.
Much as our fable-seeking selves might will it so,
not every day will be a moonwalk.

2.   Bashō in the Suburbs v5

a bullnose veranda grazes over
tessellated tiles and tuck pointing
camellias gardenias and begonias
throng the fence-line   there is a music
of the throat   in the concrete

~

cars   buses   trucks   all ants of a kind
in endless procession   stop   give way
detour   no through road   instructions
for confusion   we so immerse ourselves
in motion   stillness has grown furtive

~

the crow is the smartest of birds

it sings of distance   even when nearby
the kookaburra crowns the neighbour's stinkpipe
with a peaceful ruckus   it is pointless to quest
for certainty when one thing may mean another

Home Fires

1.   Hiding in the Daylight

The rinse-water grey finally dispelled, the sky now gleams
pure as falling snow, while the sun sniggers at this ill-fitting simile.
I am on our deck, Winnie lies snug and simpering in the chair
beside me until she erupts into a leap into the yard and a crescendo
of barking, and my eyes just catch the corn-colour legs and elongated body
of a grey crane cresting the fence-line. This has been a gala week

for birds: a king parrot sifting the offerings in Julie's lorikeet
feeding tray, the cock-bird skulking in the magnolia, and a kookaburra
and its rumbustious comedy atop a paling, also behind magnolia-camouflage,
Winnie called to heel or oblivious. Julie always counsels, "Plant them" –
westringia, kangaroo paw, grevillea, native erica – "and they will come!"
Still, the crane is a suburban alien and worthy foil for the mynas

and pigeons that have dispelled the fairy wrens; perhaps the birdbath
is the bait, though a crane cannot wade knuckle deep. For an hour a day,
we construct a newspaper, ipad and coffee hide, snug Winnie up
in a lazy blanket and keep idle time with the snare-drum throat
of a newly resident frog. This bivouac lacks serendipity's romance
and the hour soon dwindles into fractions of itself. Back in the newsreel

world, the mobile pings, there is washing on the line, crows spiral
around the aged pine across the road as the occasional car farts past,
shopping trolleys creak on the way to the mall, with a harumph,
hurried nod or wave, the radio blares at the reno sites, lorikeets pixelate
the bottlebrush, the street library welcomes mostly pensioners
and the young with mothers in tow and stillness is on day release.

Ours is a vigil for the impaling moment, a stilling of the self-chatter,
a crescendo of awareness, be it the eruption of alien feathers,
an amphibian tattoo or a parrot's counsel, infinity in a millisecond.

2.   Ours is not a through street …

                                    … though some use it so,
a ladders-and-scaffolds route to the station, the bible college
on the return loop, bus stops a right angle away, the city-bound across
a busy feeder road where we fret the old and the reckless to safety;
otherwise a haunt for locals, dog walkers and the step hungry.

The garden, in bloom with Julie's will and whimsy, affords
a grab-wreath on our realisation of the squeaky-wheeled absence
of the shopping lady, the angled tug of the trolley, its duteous distemper,
her neck a crochet hook, eyes grounded, her galumphing the muttered
inventory of her morning; wreath rethreads into a garland

should she toddle into view like a name teased from memory
after the conversation ends, linger by the street library, exchange
bush poets for detectives, a word with the gardeners or lawn men,
who trade invoices for cash-in-hand, a complicit facial plea
for the discount. "Hello, grandma!"–Julie's reblonding momentarily

abandoned too soon … but a grey mane is citizenship of the wilds,
a riposte of joy–the scamp bellows from the driveway opposite,
then galoots away on his tricycle, grin wide as an open plain.
His father mows and coaxes couch and buffalo into ordered growth,
temperate now after a childhood in the tropics, more meticulous

than prideful, his mother a wave on the way to childcare;
Wal, the previous owner, in a nursing home, as is Gwen next door,
reports from her grandson when he forsakes his console
for the light–his younger Alsatian bewails its aloneness
throughout our waking hours.
                                John, grey mane also,

shoulder-boastful, "because I can", roiling home from
the Gallipoli club, war art the pretext of his celebrations,
beard a helmet flounce when astride his retirement indulgence,
where he affects a Ulyssean pose, always left of the median line;
Christine sometimes snakes a snug pillion along his spine.

At odd times, night-fools gun their incendiary motors, cars yelp
at screeching puppies whose excitement can't be kerbed,
rattling the bottle brush into a nervous moult, bleeding
purpural funk from the crepe myrtle onto the nature strips;

in their wake the house-proud transform daylight into leaf blowers.

We are at an age when the next stage will be to shrink; we have agisted
in real estate windows, downsizer-appropriate tenements, but remain here.
Our street has no plaque, no plinth, no dolmen, no henge,
though some front-yard statuary skirts that border—our memorial
is fence-lines, the familiar, our heroism constancy, care.

Love and Hope

1.   An All Stations Train

I smooth away catkins of saliva spidering
your mouth, work to a pucker the kiss that will arc
across the distance we now endure with sweet
electricity, I pray, and not hang on your lips
like a dewlap that has outlived biological need.
To think, our embraces once rattled the bedhead!
Yours was a quizzical snare: an ardent brow, the rapture
of nomadic thought in slanting light, your hair
a gossamer weave with glints of gemstone; I yearned
to wander in that wondering. Our first meetings
were the clumsy manufactures seeming chance might allow,
your smile crinkly wry but captive, my ruses self-deceptions.
Our talk began as the shyest wren on the nethermost branch,
then trooped young and earnest into incantations,
a jig, a caper. A vase freshened with today's flowers,
not of your legacy, where I loll on sunny afternoons
but tend lacking the wise conduit of your hands,
from Abdul on the corner, whose every courtesy
is an oud; the green through the panes promises
a stroll, should I be able to wheedle you from the bed.
Meanwhile, high school poets, anchored still beneath
our octogenarian haze, as if scripted for my rusty recitals,
the headlines, the tides of nations, morsels to savour,
the tumblings and paraphernalia of the generations,
our neighbours amok. Whether these warblings make
for birdsong or settle like mist on the fixity and ache
of your gaze, I persist: your breathing is my tabernacle lamp
and, when courage shrinks, routine apes its would-be stamp.

2.   The Eternal Spring

Hope's brain centre is a dog-eared page, read inconstantly.
It resides north of the liver, south of Heaven, their neural avatars
at least, is at times more flare at sea than floodlight, more refuge
than resort; an albatross saturning the globe on thermals
and trade winds, in thrall but never subjugated, an echidna

fussing along a gumnutty track in a cleansing waft of tea tree,
a baby burbling its first smile are all occasional passers-
through, all exotherms in their departures. When cannons
gut the night, it refracts into pond spawn, not extinct
but dormant until the sky re-opens to godforsaken sense;
when fire blazes into unremitting fury, it spills hormonally
like a eucalypt pod into an ashbed vigil. Should these pinion-wheels
not turn, our lungs would infarct, our blood-beat surrender.

Words & Music, Colours & Shapes

1.   Synaesthesia

A theory for Vincent:
        his brush, his palette knife, the scumbled paint
all trembled with the world he beheld, the cascade, the thrumming,
        the plosives, the chords
        and grace notes he heard in his eyes
        in their colour-full regalia;
            his lopped ear, his death
            short circuits,
            sensory overloads.

~

Were I to paint a symphony,
        intone the colour wheel,[5] thrill an abacus
with colorimetry, then count the hues that limn our number system,
        breathe in sparks of energy,
        my poems would blaze,
        my tempos swim
            in cross-currents,
            my meanings arrive
            unlaboured.

---

[5] transliterated by Newton from spectrum to circle

2. Aphantasia

That day returns in syllables, sometimes sentence fragments,
an occasional banner headline the ghost most like an image, even
the concrete footpath buckled by fig roots is more adjectives
than angles, the edge an overhung hazard my toe found
while my eyes gloried in the tree's canopy. My head butted
the pavement as my balance fled.

Once my nights ran wild with paisley dreams, dervish faces,
sepia vignettes and truant meanings; in saner daylight,
too, an idea had to settle into a shape before I could weight it
with sense, or set it free, opposing arguments straddled
the divide like a catamaran on a fraught sea, fears
silhouetted my psyche.

I woke into a circuitry of wires, tubes, monitors, bleeps
and coruscating lights more alive than I, yet was also
sheathed in low lying fog as if a fleet of tugs and its ensemble
of warnings were shepherding the awkward and the leviathan
to restful berths or the open sea. It was when I chatted
with the nurses that I registered

this word-cast fog as mine alone. The vapours dispersed
as I recovered but never again has a clean line,
a deft sketch, a crosshatch, swatch or wisp of watercolour
flickered across the screen that is my mind, a screen made keyboard.
I know the world, can nurse its folds and notches to my skin,
sing it even, but I may as well be blind.

Singularities

Distant Discourse

With respect to Stephen Edgar

Would that a story rung from the stars
grace my eyes in an old-fashioned broadsheet
and I could expand with the universe,
whether destiny's parse
be crunch, hollow space or divine deliverance,
the story the traverse
of the voice of an inter-planetary kin
evolved from a random microbe to the fleet

peers they must comprise. We have flung
soundings into reaches we perceive
only through radio waves,
a "dialogue" begun
in hope and harmonics that now seems naïve
and scant behaves
as a confirming presence, being static
and test pattern, yet some still believe,

as if probability has congealed into fact.
I confess I, too, am an occasional glasshouse orchid
wont to stumble
weather-wracked
when the door leaks open to the realising wind
and I must acknowledge our humble
enterprise is still-born. The numbers trail
a comet of zeroes and what more could

be attempted would likely be effort wasted.
Still, what they might have told
of beginnings and transits, means and ends,
of theories basted
in a new intelligence, of dreams and plans
and what portends …
how we might have orbited beyond ourselves
released from gravity's hold.

Cinéma Grotesquerie

ensconced centre-screen   snug   smug   an aura
of empty seats beside and in front of us   feature-length
wine perched in the cup-holders in our arm rests

the ads and trailers having faded   the intro striking up
gives way to a muffled shuffling   mumbled pardon pleas
a pillowing bottom   an arrival exhalation   a cushion squelch

in the seat beside me   eyes forward   ears trying to float
above the rustle of the packet   to wander with the oboes
and violas pastelling the onscreen countryside   the creature

easing into its feedlot   a tiny pop bursting the packet edges
apart   crepitus in extracting the chips   pneumatic jaws
in mine-crush chewing   a sluice-gate slurp of Coke washing

it down   my periphery loaded with a fried, frayed scent   images
of a swollen, slavering mass who could easily devour me
the screen blazes iridescent   I contemplate slaughter

Wink

I have never witnessed the hundredth monkey at a tipping point, nor the dump truck that sorrows

in its wake, laden with a post-structuralist cargo of weighed expectations. Nor have I been one

of the twenty per cent womanfully doing the eighty who, somewhat tired, leans over after lifting,

and whose number has been trimmed by a loose cannon and the odd contagion of butterfly effect.

I am not a polymath, a universal sponge, a pathologically educative maven, nor do I rattle

like an encyclopaedia after a purgative, though I am sometimes beset with a caterpillar intensity

in this leafy world. In truth, I am more a crested macaque taking a selfie, hung out to dry after

washing its face, a poet speechless before a landmark in a watershed. It is all downhill from here.

Any Way the Wind Blows

After a stanza in "One Day's Poem" by Don Paterson

Fates are sown within it, or so the song goes,
its sea-laden form cools a cloying afternoon, we expose
our "intimate apparel" to it on good drying days, diasporas
find the four corners under its impulse, the illest variant
scorches goodness. Only the broadest wingspan bird knows,
the wandering albatross mightiest among them,
a home in its ephemera; for us
there is no harbour there, much as the carefree suppose
they'll find an anchorage. We cannot see *it*, only
its impact, and how it trembles the weather map's isobars.
Yet logic flees itself and the dream inveigles,
grows wanton even, like the very wind. We style
ourselves storm-tossed invertebrates time and again.
We call on our inner Houdinis, no doubt, to cast off
the manacles of the ordinary, to revel when we would else-while
ferment—existence has mass and the everyday
the tint of predestination.
But I wonder whether the self as leaf, the miles
a fragment must travel to embrace the whole
of nature's variegation is the root chord of our refrain.

Movement of the People[6]

our house enjoys
a north-east aspect
the sun maps
the orbit of our day

in the front bedroom
though early autumn
we have quilted the bed
and donned flannelette
yet our breakfast

on the back deck
is scarfed and hatted
by filtered sun
we linger there
when the day ahead
has not bared its teeth

our neighbours a few houses across
decamp like the circus
to FNQ and a flagrant sky
as soon as daylight saving becomes
a marginal gain   they return smug
and sun-rosed
on the trampoline of spring

down in the hollow where the street
run-off pools   those who have recently fled
Aleppo and Mogadishu huddle
our greetings are sheepishly stored
we observe the gunfire retreat by inches
from their eyes over spartan months   famine
loosen its grip on their flesh   their gazes
ascend from the gravity of suffering

in time the children
begin to badger their parents

---

[6] Derived from Hugh Dingle and V. Alistair Drake. "What Is Migration?" in *BioScience*, Volume 57, Issue 2, February 2007, p. 113-121, https://doi.org/10.1641/B570206.

to chance a pause at the street library
roll back its Aladdin door
venture an inquiring hand
withdraw a book thin with whirling colours
laughter swells beyond
the lorikeets in the bottlebrush

Subterranean Minima

a door like a seismic vent   too slight
for shoulders front on   beyond   stairs
burrowing away from daylight   another door
at the stairwell's base   a vertical rectangular
halo   exhalations of acid jazz   tempo
not time   hot & cool to equal degrees

~

a gold mine's nadiral lode   the deepest living
creature   Faust's tormentor borrowed
for its name   colloquially preternatural evil
microscopic   but its strategy a profusion
of the heat-shock proteins and resilience genes
found sparingly elsewhere   a species wormhole? [7]

~

an opera   a poem   a myth   a journey beyond
and beneath   a musician and poet   a wood nymph
a maddened flight and death by snakebite   a Lot's wife
offer once lyre and voice have unlocked the gods' tears
and the wails of the three-headed dog   the tremulous
ascent   a turned head a footfall from ecstasy

~

on the shoulders of the planet a stole
of two parts that knows both motion and heat
the one plates beneath mountain and sea   cool
the other warm   solid and fluid in the same
geologic breath   the plates move as a finger nail
and follicle grow but make and remake continents

~

---

[7] See https://cosmosmagazine.com/nature/an-in-depth-look-at-the-devil-worm/ for a discussion
of *Halicephalobus mephisto* or the devil worm.

500 days underground   carnivorous solitude
past present and future merge into mutual visions
of now   which is always 4 in the morning
sound metastasizes   becomes shamanic
peripheral vision curtails   a wasting faculty
for all this   a sense of overwhelming love[8]

~

like some semantic gravity I sink through the crust
and mantle of things toward essence   their core
the mystic seeks a hurricane stillness   my heart
is a fiery river and craves tectonic release
we all   poets included   depend on the centre
holding   without it the panorama merely adorns

---

[8] See D. T. Max, "The Woman Who Spent Five Hundred Days in a Cave", *New Yorker Magazine*, online, 21st January, 2024.

.

The Post-Modern Problem with Trolleys and Footbridges[9]

For Doctor Williams[10]
so much depended
on a red barrow,
rain-glazed and split with
precision. Also
adjacent chickens.

A runaway train
five people tied to
a railway track, one
person a spur line,
a point switch saves five,
kills one.

A runaway train
five people tied to
a railway track, one
fat man leaning over
a footbridge, push him,
save five.

Can this be
the architecture
of a moral choice?
Does so much depend
on so few details?
Would a faulty switch,

an imposed diet,
make a difference
to a moral life?
But what colours were
the point switch, the fat
man's clothes, the bridge paint?

---

[9] The Trolley and Footbridge problems were developed by Philippa Foot and Judith Jarvis
Thomson, respectively, to illustrate moral choices.
[10] Certain phrases are taken or adapted from William Carlos Williams' "The Red Wheelbarrow".

Lost for Words (*Intamooga*/Black-Footed Tree Rat)

1.
   a forest is felled
   its sawdust ploughed
   under and fed into crops
   or plaqued into housing

   an empty tree hollow
   with a once north-of-life aspect
   cindered or colonised
   by canola or architraves
   is three times absent

2.
   tinder and kindle are now bereft
   of fire   of rapture   they subsist
   in apps and devices
   and falter into seldom speech

3.
   Why is it   in loss
   we so fix on ourselves

Seed Flotsam

Costa, owl-eyes and zipper smile through the facial thicket,
　　　　brandishes a bulb, as in a tulip, daffodil or narcissus,
　　　　　　and proclaims a blueprint of the future flower at its centre.
　　　　　　　　A tangent sparks in the folds of memory, a dinner table strewn
　　　　　　　　　　with plans for a house we never build, we never inhabit.

　　　　　　　　　By eddying thought or some alchemical process,
　　　　　　when I read of the putative pistil, petal, leaf and stem,
　　　　the moisture-preserving pinafore over scales
　　that are both armature and pantry, draughtsmanship
transmutes into homunculus, that dream-kernel of a self

fit to outlive the ages, to dwell within the ineffable. I delve
　　into botanical depths, wherein not all "bulbs"
　　　　are common lore bulbs, some more properly
　　　　　　inflorescent corms, tubers with rooting eyes
　　　　　　　　or rhizomes desperately seeking sideways, think crocus,

　　　　　　　　dahlia or iris, all *pirouettes en dehors* of evolution.
　　　　　　The mind-eddies quicken into rapids, a light bulb
　　　　moment jostles with rootstock, analogy flounders.
　　A poem at some level renders mind geography to scale
while, elbow deep in soil, semantics redound in a gardener's toil.

Ornithorhynchus Paradoxus

Bird/reptile/mammal/"living fossil".

Skin and sketch sent back,
labelled a fraudulent collage cut
from other species—became
a scissor-scarred museum pelt;
"high frolic", everything "queer
and opposite" in that
"zoological penal colony".

The *Beagle*, a fleeting visit,
a chain of ponds, an evening
pungent with observation,
its conflicted pontificator:
"Surely two Creators
must have been at work!"

~

Satin water, a ripple
on the pond surface:
a whispered spinnaker
in profile, as if spun
from a prayer wheel;
sail-shape-snub-nose
pointed at the farther shore,
never arriving,
fading diagonals;
a litany of gums
in the lifting veil.
The loss for a second
of that sliver of bill
and nostril, its tawny slick,
mists my binoculars.

A Defiant Cosmos

Galileo was forced to abjure his belief in the heliocentrism of Copernicus
by the Holy Inquisition under threat of torture.

The ocean of night is awash with petals and sprays
of light. Though I peer through a naive tube fraught
with mirrors, there is spark enough for both wonder
and calculation, the latter should my failing eyes
consent. Before, I placed this scope so images were cast
on the parchment I had set below it and I traced
the shadowed patterns with charcoal, a cartoon
of the immeasurable. (An apparent paradox, no more.)
The Creator turns all, counts as gnats our squabbles
as to the Sun or Earth as axis, the other in orbiting thrall,
yet shares His auspices everywhere to inch us towards
knowledge. Yes, I recanted to spare myself Bruno's flames[11]
but *sotto voce* screamed *"eppur si muove"*[12] to the silence
that comprehends, the mind that is the spheres.

---

[11] Giardono Bruno was burned at the stake for heresy.

[12] "And yet it moves".

Uberrimae Fidei[13]

A boardroom at eagle height,
a plate-glass panorama,

skiffs and eighteen footers duel
in aquamarine, the wind fuel
to a scuffed harbour, whisps of foam
like ancient eyebrows beneath foreheads
of rumpled staves, The Beach Boys'
"Sloop John B", a trilling flute,

strange harmonics in my tinnitus.
The agenda is mired in the sweaty tarmac
of pricing: profit, fairness and trade-offs.
Even the crispest minds have tacky feet.

A navy supply ship, fleet grey, an out-of-context
gatekeeper except when history interjects
and older heads recall ships in plural,
crowded streets, uniforms, 60s R&R,
the Whisky-Au-GoGo. Mid-window,
the Botanical Gardens smile unobtrusively.

Questions of degree are the hardest
to parse: facts bow before hunches
and assertion roosters as reason.

The city rerises in the east, a slalom descent
to wealth, further on the unfussed ferment,
oil-smeared, salt-crusted, sand-toed,
biting into paper bags, the waves an ageless call
to mammals to return to the sea.

We move on, uncontent
but unbereft, knowing we will rewalk
this labyrinth. I rise from the timber table
shaped into an ellipse, woozy
with the opinions orbiting
the room, then steady myself

and my eyes fill with the entire atlas,
the earlier tableaux its maps
merged and rectangular, a Mercator projection,
perspectived, yet shamanic, seeming
within an arm's embrace.

In this world of Janus trades—the near,
the far, the part, the whole, the everyday,
the rarefied, the trustee, the beneficiary,
the governing, the governed,
the few, the many—at one end a duty
and pledge, the other hope seamed with suspicion.

---

[13] The legal principle of utmost good faith.

The Author

Paul Scully is a Sydney-based poet, an actuary by training and works part-time in finance. He holds a Masters in Creative Writing and is a Doctor of Arts from the University of Sydney. *The Literate Detective and Other Crimes* is his fourth published poetry collection. His first, *An Existential Grammar* (Walleah Press), was short-listed for the Anne Elder Award. His poetry has been commended and short-listed in major Australian poetry competitions, including the ACU and Newcastle Poetry Prizes, and has been published in print and online journals in Australia, Ireland, the UK and USA. His website is http://www.paulscullypoet.com.au/.

Also by Paul Scully

An Existential Grammar
Suture Lines
The Fickle Pendulum

Notes

Notes

Notes

Notes

Notes

Notes

Notes

www.ingramcontent.com/pod-product-compliance
Lightning Source LLC
Chambersburg PA
CBHW051557030426
42334CB00034B/3467